JACQUI A. S

I DECIDED

From Resolution to Execution

Diligence Excellence Confidence Integrity Discipline Enthusiasm Dedication

Proven Steps to Move from Resolution to Execution

DEDICATION

Dedicated to the Memory of

Rosie Showers, my Mother, who encouraged me when others didn't believe in me and told me to "prove them wrong." That advice continues to encourage me to keep moving forward regardless of the obstacles or the "they says" of the world.

Patricia Holmes Ellison, my beloved sister and best friend forever, who would always say, "Jacqui, just make a decision!"

Dedicated to

LeEtta Holmes Pye, my niece-daughter, who I encourage every day to make decisions that will propel her to achieve greatness and experience the abundant life God envisioned for her.

All my family and friends who prayed and encouraged me through the process of writing this book.

TABLE OF CONTENTS

Douglas!
Decide to
Succeed!
Envisioned you succeeding!
Before you were born!
Blessing to ya!
[signature] 8/12/20

PREFACE

R esolutions are a tradition that we observe every year. Sometimes we're not sure why we do them, but we find ourselves doing them nevertheless. More often than not, we don't get past January before we have broken them. And in some instances, we don't get beyond writing them. Well, I was no different from probably millions of people in the world. After realizing that more than 10-plus years had passed and I was still writing the same resolutions, I got tired. At that moment, I made the decision that I wasn't going to write another one. Why? I wasn't committed to making them happen.

I knew I needed to decide to be committed to my resolutions, or I would never be successful in making those resolutions a reality. One day I sat down and started thinking about what would cause me to be committed to the vows I wrote every year. I realized that if I didn't have a transformation in how I viewed the resolutions, I would never be successful. Because I knew I had to make a decision, I arbitrarily selected the word DECIDED. From there I thought about what it would take for me to be successful. What ingredients did I need to put together to help me move from just writing resolutions to actually completing them?

As I pondered DECIDED, I started writing down the words that I felt would be critical to my success. Success is rooted in what you are willing to do every day. If I was not willing to be committed to doing something every day, I was never going to be able to do more than just write resolutions. My success was contingent upon my daily routine or being committed to doing something every day. The first "D" was for diligence to keep me focused on establishing a daily routine of just doing it.

Anyone who knows me knows that I want things done right. I won't say that I'm a perfectionist, but I'm close. Instead of looking at myself as a perfectionist, that doesn't have much room for error, I adopted the word excellence. Regardless, if I was successful or not I knew I had given it my best. That is the difference. Excellence enables you to do what you do without the pressure of perfectionism. If you don't succeed there is no guilt because you gave it your best. The second letter "E" had to be for excellence.

Over the years I battled my way out of fear, especially when it came to my writing. For me to be successful, confidence in my capabilities was critical. So many, including me, don't have confidence in their God-given talents and gifts. Oftentimes, they never fight for those gifts. I fought to write. I fought to have confidence in what was given to me by God. Every day I knew I had to remind myself of that confidence, not just for writing, but for anything I wanted to do in life. So, I needed a "C" for confidence.

One thing that was obvious is that I had become a habitual bearer of untruths, especially to myself and about myself. Year after year, when I wrote those resolutions without the least bit of commitment to fulfilling them, it spoke volumes about my integrity. Although I

2   I DECIDED

claimed I was prepared to make those changes that was not the truth. Even while I was writing them, there was dishonesty because I had no plan or strategy to execute them. Needless to say, "I" needed some integrity that would force me to be committed to the vows and resolutions I was making to myself. "I" for integrity was needed.

I can't tell you how many times I gave myself a pep talk. I was eloquent and sincere, or so I thought, but as soon as that pep rally was over whatever routine I was trying to goad myself into doing didn't get done. For some reason, I couldn't figure out why I was not accomplishing anything or being successful. There was a lack of control of my time, resources and more. Not achieving my resolutions or goals was indicative of not being disciplined enough to see them through. You must be able to say "No" and especially to yourself. Saying no, or even yes, can be hard. Success is in my daily routine. Without a daily prescription for success, none of those resolutions were going to happen. That is when I adopted the "D" for discipline. It has made all the difference in the world.

I knew I had to be enthusiastic about every goal I wanted to accomplish. Viewing each goal as a daunting task was not going to be beneficial as I set out to transform my behavior and become a finisher. My attitude was critical to being successful in accomplishing my goals. If I felt that I couldn't do it, then I was not going to be able to do it. Regardless of the obstacles, my attitude toward those obstacles would determine my ability to overcome them. My enthusiasm catapulted me above the worry and anxiety that could have easily prevented me from overcoming them. I quickly learned that worrying about the obstacles was not going to get me any closer to completing my goals. Being excited about every goal would help to bolster my confidence, determination and dedication about achieving my goals. So, "E" had to be for Enthusiasm.

I unequivocally knew my success was contingent upon being dedicated and determined to be a finisher. I wrestled with those two words—dedication and determination. Yet, I knew that I needed them both for me to progress toward the fulfillment of my goals. Ultimately, my dedication to not just writing the goals down, but for them to become an integral part of my life would make me determined to succeed.

Commitment to most things has always been a challenge for me, but to jump over the hurdle of non-success I had to get over my phobia of commitment. Knowing this, enabled me to become dedicated to respecting the vows I made to myself. If I could not be dedicated to the vows or goals I set for myself, there was no way I could be committed to those I made to anyone else. In espousing to this principle, no longer could I allow myself to write my resolutions down and do nothing about them. Even God made himself accountable by swearing the promise on Himself. If God, who is the Creator of all things, could do that I know I can do it too because of His Spirit that resides inside of me. Dedication and determination collided in thrusting me forward as I moved from just being a doer to being a finisher. "D" was identified for Dedication.

Embracing these principles, I experienced a transformation in my life. Those resolutions began to move me into execution with each passing year. I want you to know that it didn't happen overnight. It has taken many years and hard work. I prayed. I fasted. I consecrated myself for success. You must be willing to make the same commitment for your success. Believe me, you are going to need a power greater than you to garner the strength necessary to endure as you move all the way from resolution to execution.

It has been worth it. I took off my pretty red dress, put on my old dirty overalls and worked hard. That is what success is all about—hard work. There is no way around it.

Along the way, I faced my vulnerabilities and my fears. If you are not willing to face your fears, you will never be able to move from resolution to execution. Every day I talk with people who find themselves stuck for whatever reason. Many are just like I was. They know what they should be doing, but they haven't been able to do it.

Everything is written down and ready to go, but they are just mere words on paper. You read them, but they have not become a part of you. Until those words become a part of you and you truly make a commitment to accomplish them, success will elude you. Intimately embrace them until what is written down, that appears to be pipe dreams, becomes your reality. You begin to feel and know that you are worthy for them to happen. For instance, I was amazed at how much content people had on their blogs and websites. As I began to embrace the worthiness of my dreams to become a reality, I experienced from others how I felt. I never fathomed that one day, people would express the same sentiments about me that I had felt about others.

One day I started writing my way out of fear. You see, I was afraid of writing. I definitely was afraid to allow people to see what I had written. I feared their judgment. So, I didn't write! I always loved writing until my first journalism class at Wayne State University. What I perceived to be words from a professor to dissuade me, years later I realized were words to inspire and motivate me to hone my gift and never give up. To prove him wrong, I was determined that I was not going to give up because in the crevices of my soul I knew there was a good writer with much to say. Interestingly enough, my anger and frustration at him actually caused me to fervently study grammar to overcome my writing deficiencies.

Several years ago, I felt an intense prompting to write a weekly inspirational message. Even amid the fear, I did it. Heeding that inner voice was one of the most liberating acts I have ever done. I have been committed to writing a weekly e-blast that became a blog and is now evolving into a book. A few years after that, I began to write a daily prayer which will be compiled into a book as well. Moving from resolution to execution requires making a decision. My commitment to writing unequivocally exemplifies my decision to move into action. My diligence has paid off as I gained confidence in my abilities, and the courage to become dedicated to using them.

I still write resolutions. Now, I am an executor of them. It is in the execution of the resolution that I found me. I found my courage. I found my confidence. I found my voice. I was no longer afraid to decide to move forward with my goals. I was no longer afraid to peer deep into the fissures of my fear and emerge fearless. Life for me has never been the same. I hope that as you read, ponder and adopt these seven principles, it will never be the same for you.

In the search for an impetus to forge me from resolution to execution I adopted a credo that spurred me to accomplish what I had not been able to accomplish. I have been liberated ever since. Whenever I find myself not fulfilling my goals, or resolutions, I have a creed to reinforce my commitment to forge ahead and do what needs to be done. I DECIDED to exercise Diligence, Excellence, Confidence, Integrity, Discipline, Enthusiasm and Dedication and to live by a credo that would propel me into accomplishing the untapped resolutions I had set for myself year after year. This credo continues to be a guidepost for me as I have successfully moved from resolution to execution. It is my hope and prayer that it will be the same for you.

INTRODUCTION

One year I made a conscious decision that I was not going to write down a list of goals for the ensuing year. In the past, I would always make sure when the clock turned over another year to have my goals in hand praying over them and believing that when the year had ended I would have completed them all. Just like every other year, I was nowhere near completing those goals when the year came to an end. Rummaging through papers while cleaning out the clutter, I kept running across the same list of goals. The only difference was the date noted. Year after year, many of those goals had not changed. Oh yes, many were yet to be fulfilled. Instantly I realized I didn't need to write these resolutions down again, I needed to execute them.

My relationship with these goals had to be transformed and I had to respect them. For the goals to truly become reality, my mind-set had to change about them. Mere words on paper do not breed success. True success is only achieved when the words jump off the paper and begin to run toward the finish line with a determination to never give up until what it set out to do has been achieved. This happens when the decision is made that you no longer will give lip service, but that you will be actively and intimately involved in making it happen.

As I read over many years of written goals I experienced an "ah-ha" moment. Obviously, I had perfected the art of writing resolutions; but I needed to perfect my ability to execute them. At that point, I made the decision not to write another goal without completing those that had already been written. My dilemma was not writing resolutions; I had mastered that. My dilemma was executing and completing them.

Essentially, the goals needed to move from my hands into my heart. I had to be passionate and committed to the goals to achieve them. It was then that I developed the mantra, "I DECIDED".

It was the decision to no longer be caught up in an exercise of futility by writing goals that would never be achieved. Actually, the goals were written, I just never came back to them until it was time to write them again the following year. This vicious cycle repeated itself year after year. I wrote the goals. Prayed over them. Then, tucked them away until it was time to write them again the following year.

I re-evaluated the goals with the express intention of establishing the right relationship with each resolution to accomplish them. We're talking about a decade or more of the same goals gathering dust, waiting to not just be achieved, but for someone to respect and care enough to act on them.

Something different needed to happen; a fire needed to be ignited inside of me. It was not working well for me to continuously write those goals year after year and a different approach was needed for me to be successful. After deliberating over what was needed for true transformation to take place, "I DECIDED" emerged as the motivation for me to move past just mere words on paper, to achieve them. It had to become a part of the very essence of my being every single day.

It was obvious I had not made a true commitment to the goals because not only were they never achieved, but I didn't respect them or the process. If you never truly commit to the goals, how in the world do you ever plan to execute them? You don't, and I didn't. If you never respect them, there is absolutely no way you will be committed to them. Moving from resolution to execution, I had to understand why I wasn't achieving them or why I was less than half-heartedly committed to achieving them. This glass was nowhere near half empty, it was just plain bone dry.

What became crystal clear was that my mind-set prevented me from truly achieving the goals, because I had not truly made up in my mind that the goals were achievable or even important. I wrote those resolutions, but I didn't believe in them. How in the world can anything become a reality if you don't believe in it? It can't! The only way I could begin to believe in my goals was to take a transparent look at why I continually missed the mark. In my heart of hearts, I knew I had good intentions, but when it was time for execution I fell vastly short of the target.

Oftentimes we do things just to be doing them. Because someone said you need to write resolutions at the beginning of the year, we do it! More often than not a lot of thought or planning does not go into it. It is an exercise of futility that appears to be the right thing to do. That is the reason why most people who make New Year's resolutions falter within the first month. Many never make it out of January and some never make it past the first week or even the first day.

Resolutions should not be haphazardly made; you truly have to ponder them. One of the biggest considerations is you. If you never truly decide that you are going to accomplish your resolutions, you will never be successful in executing the corresponding actions for your success. If you are not true to yourself and the fulfillment of your goals, why would you even write them down?

Fulfilling goals far exceeds just writing them down. It is an ever-evolving process that drives you forward. Your attitude is only to write them down, but if you never envision the process to fulfilling them, then you are already defeated before you start.

With every goal, there is a three-prong process: a launching pad, incremental steps to get there and finally achieving the goal. Your mind-set toward the start and the incremental steps makes all the difference in your success.

"For better or for worse, your destiny is the result of your daily decisions and defining decisions. If you make good decisions on a daily basis, it has a cumulative effect that pays dividends for the rest of your life. Along with daily decisions, there are defining decisions. We only make a few defining decisions in life, and then we spend the rest of our lives managing them. Never underestimate the potential of one resolution to change your life." (Batterson 2011, 170-171).

Goals, once often set, are not achieved because the mind-set is never changed about what needs to be done for them to be achievable. There comes a time when our faith in our goals is kept ignited by our diligent actions between the start and the finish. This can only happen when you transform your thoughts for you to transform your actions.

"The hand of the diligent maketh rich."
Proverbs 10:4 (King James Version).

Habakkuk 2:2 (King James Version), exhorts to "write the vision, and make it plain..." The subsequent verse says to be patient in the process even when it appears as though the vision is delayed. Writing the vision is the initial step in the process. Sometimes when it appears the vision is not being fulfilled, you cannot give up on it. The vision has to be as detailed as possible to enable you to endure the process of accomplishing the vision. The more detailed the vision, the better able you will be to achieve it. A vision with milestones for success enables you to celebrate the goals reached within the "final/overall goal". These incremental milestones of celebration will bolster your commitment to completing the overall goal.

There comes a time when taking an authentic look inward enables you to ascertain why your resolutions are not coming to fruition. It is through this inner work that true change takes place. Looking at the fears that have prevented you from executing your resolutions is a big step in the right direction. Confronting them with confidence and courage is critical. If you are not afraid to confront those emotions, you will experience success. Once you confront them, then you will begin to tackle them. In tackling them, you will be able to move from resolution to execution. This is the credo I adopted to move from resolution to execution—I DECIDED to exercise Diligence, Excellence, Confidence, Integrity, Discipline, Enthusiasm and Dedication. The goals have been set. Now it is time to run with Diligence, Excellence, Confidence, Integrity, Discipline, Enthusiasm and Dedication to achieve them. You see, the only way to move past a situation and conquer the fear that appears to conquer you is to acknowledge its existence and map out a strategy to overcome it. I had to take a long hard introspective look at myself and ask why I could not uphold the vows I had made to myself. I determined that the vows were never completed because I was unwilling to put forth the necessary effort to make them happen. Fear was at the crux of it all and overcoming that fear in all of its complexities had to be the guiding force that would lead me through the process. That will also guide you through the process as well.

chapter one

DILIGENCE

Diligent Hands Make Me Rich

S uccess is always linked to our daily routine. Nothing else will make you as successful as diligence. I know numerous people with intelligence beyond measure, yet they lacked the diligence to do what it took for them to be successful. Diligence did not complement their intellect and their intellect did not complement diligence for their success. I was no different. I wrote those resolutions each year with the intention of completing them as I clutched them in my hands praying the old year out and the New Year in with a vow, yet again, to fulfill a myriad of resolutions. These resolutions, for the most part, were already abandoned before New Year's Day ended–probably before it even started. I never had a real plan of action to achieve them.

In the cleft of my consciousness they existed, but in my everyday life they did not. I was not doing my due diligence to make them happen. Yet, at the end of the year I would wonder why I didn't achieve them, but I kept rewriting the resolutions anyways. A diligent hand is what brings you into the flow of success.

What you do every single day determines your success. You cannot haphazardly meander from one day to the next without working on your goals. It doesn't work that way. You have to make a conscious decision that every single day you are going to do something that brings you closer to it. It begins with planning. How can you be diligent without a plan?

I want to stress that it is more than just writing the plan, you must be committed to executing the plan as well. You write the vision and if you allow it to do what it is meant to do, it will propel you forward day after day. If you only write it and not embrace it as you run passionately to fulfill it, you will not be successful. Success is always linked to your daily routine. When I speak of routine it has nothing to do with the boredom of repetitive tasks that do not bring much pleasure. It means passionately pursuing your goals with a commitment to succeed every single day, and putting forth the corresponding actions that lead to success.

Transforming your mind-set about routine tasks for you to become successful is always the starting place. This can be applied to anything in your life. If you view it as routine, you will not be able to muster up what is necessary for you to do. After a few days, boredom will set in and you will not be able to do anything. You will abandon the process.

For example, I was not the best housekeeper for many years. When I did clean my house, it was done extremely well, but it did not last. Before long, things were back in disarray just as before and the task appeared just as insurmountable. I had to muster up enough energy to tackle the daunting task of housecleaning, once again.

While visiting a friend when her father passed away, I found myself observing her housekeeping practices. I noticed she cleaned constantly. Not like I would always do, spending an entire day cleaning because things just got out of hand. She made sure everything was put back into its place and she washed the dishes as soon as they were dirty. These were simple things she did in keeping her house neat and tidy. She wasn't exhausted as I would be because she labored all day to get things clean and back in their places.

Well, I adopted her way of doing things. Every day I realized I had to do something to keep my house neat, tidy and guest ready. No longer do I have to apologize when people come to visit unexpectedly. Yes, this was one of those resolutions that I wrote down year after year. Not until I respected diligence, and yes, cleanliness, was I able to overcome slothfulness.

It is no different in any other area of your life. The diligent reaps the rewards inherent in a daily routine of just doing whatever you need to do. The same commitment to diligence is true for your business, finances, health, etc. I want to emphasize why diligence is so important, it is critical to your success. Without being determined to succeed every single day, you will be just like I was: stuck in between resolution and execution. You will never achieve the level of success that you desire. I want you to be a success. You deserve to become and achieve everything you were created for.

Whatever habits you have been using in the past and you have not been successful, it is apparent that you need to release them. Analyze where you have been putting your energies and if it does not inspire you to accomplish your goals, abandon them right now. Decide that those bad habits can no longer be a part of your daily routine. You must be committed to doing something every single day to reach your goals. That commitment has to be those positive habits that move you in the right direction. If not, you won't be successful.

Determine what your daily routine will be. Eliminate those things that are not beneficial to your success. Incorporate those things that will bring you to the success you desire to achieve. It begins and ends with you and your commitment to your daily routine.

If you have not created a plan of action, then you definitely will not be successful. Take the time each day to write down what you want to accomplish. You need an annual plan with actionable steps for you to become an executor of success. This annual plan must be broken down by month, week, day and (in some cases) hour. Having a detailed outline will help your commitment to diligence.

This is probably one of the most critical areas in moving from resolution to execution. Initially, it may appear to be an arduous and daunting task, but before long it will become second nature. I'm amazed at how quickly I wash dishes or even clean. I began respecting the daily routine of these tasks by just doing them. To be successful in every area of your life, you have to respect the discipline of diligence. You must respect the discipline of the daily routine and be committed to it or you will look up at the end of the year with a fistful of resolutions and no accomplishments.

INTROSPECTIVE REFLECTIONS

What habits do you need to eliminate?

_____

_____

_____

Did you know that success is in your daily routine?

_____

_____

_____

Do you map out a daily plan of action to keep you moving forward?

_____

_____

_____

Do you respect the discipline of the daily routine?

_____

_____

_____

PURPOSEFUL MEDITATIONS

"...but the hand of the diligent maketh rich."
Proverbs 10:4 (King James Version).

_"And the LORD answered me, and said, Write the vision,
and make it plain upon tables, that he may run that readeth it.
For the vision is yet for an appointed time, but at the end
it shall speak, and not lie: though it tarry, wait for it;
because it will surely come, it will not tarry."_
Habakkuk 2:2-3 (King James Version).

*"So teach us to number our days, that we may
apply our hearts unto wisdom."*
Psalm 90:12 (King James Version).

*"If one advances confidently in the direction
of his dreams, and endeavors to live the life which
he has imagined, he will meet with a success
unexpected in common hours."* (Thoreau 1854).

*"Therefore do not cast away your confidence, which
has great reward. For you have need of endurance,
so that after you have done the will of God,
you may receive the promise."*
Hebrews 10:35-36 (New King James Version).

PRAYER OF DECISION

*Father, My diligent hands make me rich. My commitment
to success begins with my doing something every single day.
I am committed to being diligent as You teach me how
to number my days as I apply my heart to wisdom.
Amen.*

NOTES

NOTES

I DECIDED

chapter two

EXCELLENCE

Embrace Excellence

M y first job in Washington D.C. was with a magazine publishing company. In that position, I developed the skills and expertise that infused me with a spirit of excellence that I continue to cultivate. I experienced firsthand that when you strive for excellence, you are unstoppable and experience tremendous success. Sometimes it was annoying and tedious to do what seemed to be mundane tasks. I quickly learned that respecting the smallest of details made the difference between mediocrity and excellence. It was the difference between something being ordinary or extraordinary.

My boss forced us to analyze the minutest of details and this same commitment to detail saturated that company. It truly made a difference. That commitment to excellence propelled that company to overtake its major competitor within a matter of years and position itself as a major influencer in the magazine publishing industry. I continue to draw from that experience even today.

The two owners of that magazine publishing company were driven by setting themselves apart from their competitor. They didn't have nearly the financial resources their competitor did, but they adopted a spirit of excellence that resulted in them becoming a multimillion dollar company within a few years. That same spirit was imparted to each employee—I know it was definitely imparted to me.

Over the years I've been told that I am a perfectionist. I unequivocally denied it. You see, I didn't perceive myself as a perfectionist. However, there probably was some truth to that statement because perfectionism causes you to procrastinate and I was a huge procrastinator. Perfectionists can't quite get started because they feel that whatever they do will not be their best. So, they do nothing and never know what their best could have been. Their "best" eludes them.

When you strive for excellence you may sometimes fall short of your goal, but you don't need to stay down. You get up, assess your mistakes and keep moving forward. A perfectionist lives in constant condemnation and fear. However, when you strive for excellence you realize that God gave someone the wisdom to invent erasers because he knew that in the process of getting where He intended for us to go, we would make some mistakes. Procrastinators are often paralyzed by their mistakes. Those who operate with a spirit of excellence view their mistakes as opportunities enabling them to succeed.

I've come to realize that excellence enables you not to despise the days of small beginnings. You see, it is in the small beginnings where God is perfecting you to be what He's called you to be.

I DECIDED

I haven't always been very comfortable with that notion. In many instances, I did nothing because I was afraid that whatever I did was not going to be as spectacular as I had hoped. It was easier to do nothing. It appeared to be safer when in actuality it was a cowardly act. God has taught me through experience not to give up and to do it anyway, regardless of the outcome or the imminent fear.

You will never realize your full potential if you do not adopt a spirit of excellence. Mediocrity impedes innovation and prevents you from walking in your true purpose. Excellence sets you apart for greatness and enables you to move swiftly in the direction to fulfill your goals. Unfortunately, far too many people have settled for just enough, barely enough or not enough. Mediocrity has a crippling effect because it states that you are not worthy of anything. If you feel you are not worthy, then you will settle for less and not feel you are worthy to strive for more. Day after day you will find yourself in the same place hoping for more, but not willing to put forth the corresponding efforts to achieve it.

People of excellence are envied and may be called snobbish, because others who have elected not to operate in excellence label them as such. Rather than making a decision to embrace an excellent spirit at work, home, church and your community, many have elected to sit on the sidelines and make malicious comments about those who have. You can't get caught up in trying to please them while being distracted from reaching your goals. Evaluate the relationships for what they are and in many instances, you have to let them go. If you don't, then the same mediocre attitude they possess will begin to possess you. If you want more, then go after more and leave those who don't want more where they are. No, you are not being snobbish you are determined to succeed. In that determination, you have to recognize those who don't want to put forth the effort and leave them be.

From the beginning of time, we have operated on the principle of seedtime and harvest. Whatever you sow you shall reap. If you sow mediocrity you will receive less than average results. However, if you sow excellence you will be outstanding in the field and your harvest will be in abundance. As we read in Scripture, Daniel and Joseph sowed excellence and they were able to experience freedom that most people never experience, even though they were in captivity.

Excellence is an attitude reflected in all you do. Diligence coupled with a spirit of excellence yields an abundant harvest of success. People who do just enough, never experience the fullness God has for them. Just enough will yield you "a just enough" harvest. A fervent spirit of excellence moves you to another plateau of wealth, abundance, graciousness, blessing and favor.

At some point, you make the decision to no longer operate in the sphere of mediocrity. In essence, every minute of every day is used for His glory. In all you do, understand that being diligent and exhibiting excellence has to do with whom you work for 24 hours a day, seven days a week. Once you understand who you work for it doesn't matter what you do, you will do it with a spirit of excellence to be pleasing to your audience of One—*God Himself.*

INTROSPECTIVE REFLECTIONS

Do you do everything with a spirit of excellence?

_____

_____

_____

Have you decided to get rid of the mediocrity in your life?

_____

_____

What can you do to embrace and adopt a spirit of excellence in everything that you do?

_____

_____

_____

PURPOSEFUL MEDITATIONS

*"He that hath knowledge spareth his words: and
a man of understanding is of an excellent spirit."*
Proverbs 17:27 (King James Version).

*"If you are going to achieve excellence in big things,
you develop the habit in little matters."*
General Colin Powell (Famous Quotes at BrainyQuote n.d.).

*"Perfection is not attainable, but if we chase perfection we can
catch excellence."* Vince Lombardi (Inside The Huddle n.d.).

PRAYER OF DECISION

*Father, For far too long I have operated well below my sphere
of potential, because I have been consumed with achieving
perfection. Bless me with a spirit of excellence. Because You are
my divine Creator and placed in me a most excellent spirit.
Teach me how to adopt excellence in every area of my life.
All I do, I will perform with a spirit of excellence as I glorify
You in the marketplace.
Amen.*

NOTES

I DECIDED

chapter three

CONFIDENCE
I Will Not Cast Away My Confidence

"I can't do it!" "It's too hard!" "I don't know what I'm doing!" "I'm too young!" "I'm too old!" "I don't have enough experience." These diminutive words are confidence busters. Whenever people say they can't do something it is because they are afraid. Once they're able to confront the fear, they can rise above the confidence busters. As long as they hide behind them, they will never achieve their goals and experience the success they desire. Holding fast to your confidence is critical for you to move into a place of execution.

Several years ago, I realized the problem preventing me from succeeding, had to do with my lack of confidence in my capabilities. You can have confidence in one area and not have confidence in another. It wasn't that I didn't know what to do, but I didn't have enough confidence in the knowledge, wisdom and understanding I had garnered from my years of experience.

I found myself not being able to move past a certain level of achievement, because I didn't have the confidence in my ability to accomplish whatever I set out to do.

This is the position of many. It is not that they don't know or cannot learn; the problem is that they do not have the confidence in their innate and learned abilities to be successful. Sure, you may make some mistakes along the way—that is all a part of the success walk. If you don't make mistakes, you will never learn. If you allow them, the mistakes you make can increase your confidence and become one of the major catalysts for you to move from resolution to execution. With every mistake you make, you will assess what worked and what didn't. From this assessment, you will do either one of two things. You will do nothing, or You will proceed confidently in another direction or make the necessary adjustments for success. If you do the latter, you will build your confidence because you will have taken the time to learn, which in turn bolsters your confidence to keep increasing your knowledge base.

As Solomon was on the threshold of becoming King of Israel, his father David instructed him not to be afraid. He told him that God would be with him every step of the way, he would supply all of the resources he will need, and no matter what to just do whatever God instructs him to do. All he had to do was have confidence and to not be discouraged nor afraid. You see, fear brings torment and discouragement. It causes you not to do what you have been created to do. When you allow fear into one area of your life, it will try to invade those areas where you already have confidence. You must make the decision that fear will not be the controlling force that prevents you from doing what you know you need to do. Lack of confidence is always embedded in fear. To supersede its grip, you have to embrace confidence.

Confidence is rooted in faith. It is hard not to be confident when you have faith to believe that whatever you set out to do you will accomplish it. If you don't have that faith, you will second-guess yourself and always question your capabilities. Even though you know that you are capable, a lack of faith will cause you to be anxious and prevent you from being successful.

Everything you need to be successful is already inside of you. Once you realize God has already supplied you with everything you need it becomes easier for you to do it with confidence and courage. Howbeit fear will be there, but your confidence in your capabilities will enable you to overcome the inherent fear.

While I was working for an association there was a young woman who was promoted to an advertising sales position because she had functioned exceptionally well as an administrative assistant. Three weeks before the ad closing date she had only sold one ad. Day after day she would sit in her office not knowing what to do. She was too afraid to ask for help because she didn't want anyone to know she didn't have a clue about what needed to be done. She lacked the confidence to get the job done, and even more, to ask for help.

I knew she could do the job and tried to encourage her in innumerable ways. It became obvious that the task to encourage her was bigger, because she had to overcome her lack of confidence in not only her capabilities but also her lack of confidence in herself. When I queried her about her positive attributes she couldn't think of one. I was amazed! And yet, I could rattle off numerous positive character traits about this young woman.

Needless to say, she didn't meet the advertising goal and was terminated. Along the way, I encouraged her to have confidence in those things that she did well, and that confidence would overflow into those things that she didn't.

I found out that she dropped out of college when she was only one year away from obtaining her degree. After she was let go from that job, we continued to stay in contact with each other. I would constantly encourage her to go back to school. She finally returned. She not only received her bachelor's degree, but she went on to obtain her master's degree as well.

How can you have confidence if you never take the first step because you are afraid of failing? The Scriptures exhort us not to cast away our confidence, because it is our confidence that allows us to reap the manifold benefits God has for our lives as long as we do not give up Hebrews 10:35 (New King James Version). Confidence enables you to endure and exercise diligence in your endurance. As you move forward in acquiring wisdom it enhances your confidence to know that the very things that you were once afraid to do, you will be able to do them. Confidence bolsters your self-esteem until you no longer feel that you are unworthy to reap the blessing and favor of God.

True confidence comes when you connect with the source of all confidence—The Almighty God. It is then you will know God equipped you with the confidence and courage to be a success in all your endeavors. It is then that you can confidently and courageously move from resolution to execution.

INTROSPECTIVE REFLECTIONS

In what areas do you lack confidence? Do you know why?

_____

_____

_____

Are you willing to do what is necessary to become more confident and courageous in your capabilities and yourself?

_____

_____

_____

PURPOSEFUL MEDITATIONS

"Cast not away therefore your confidence, which hath great recompence of reward. For ye have need of patience, that, after ye have done the will of God, ye might receive the promise." Hebrews 10:35-36 (King James Version).

"And David said to Solomon his son, Be strong and of good courage, and do it: fear not, nor be dismayed: for the LORD God, even my God, will be with thee; he will not fail thee, nor forsake thee, until thou hast finished all the work for the service of the house of the LORD." 1 Chronicles 28:20 (King James Version).

"If one advances confidently in the direction of his dreams, and endeavors to live the life which he has imagined, he will meet with a success unexpected in common hours." (Thoreau 1854).

"Have not I commanded thee? Be strong and of a good courage; be not afraid, neither be thou dismayed: for the LORD thy God is with thee whithersoever thou goest."
Joshua 1:9 (King James Version).

Prayer of Decision

Father, I will no longer lack confidence in my capabilities. Bless me to overcome overwhelming fear that prevents me from moving forward knowing that You have already equipped me for great success. Bless me not to walk in a double-minded state questioning my ability to fulfill my assignments. As I walk confidently in the purpose you have ordained, bless me not to lean to my own understanding, but to always acknowledge You as the source of my wisdom, understanding, counsel, might and knowledge.
Amen.

NOTES

_____
_____
_____
_____
_____
_____
_____
_____
_____
_____
_____
_____
_____
_____
_____
_____
_____
_____
_____
_____
_____
_____
_____
_____
_____
_____
_____
_____

NOTES

_____
_____
_____
_____
_____
_____
_____
_____
_____
_____
_____
_____
_____
_____
_____
_____
_____
_____
_____
_____
_____
_____
_____
_____
_____
_____
_____
_____
_____

I DECIDED

chapter four

INTEGRITY
Walk in Your Integrity

The church I grew up in always conducted what was referred to as "testimony service". During testimony service, people shared a testimony of trial or triumph with the congregation. It was customary when you testified to begin by acknowledging others and saying, "I give honor to the Pastor, his wife..." or whomever you wanted to recognize.

I was about twelve years old and longed to have someone recognize and honor me. So, I asked one of the young boys to give me honor when it was his turn to testify. He did it!

Almost immediately people started laughing. I, on the other hand, didn't see anything wrong. I felt quite important because I was recognized and given honor in front of everyone. It didn't matter that I had to ask someone to do it. It didn't even matter if I deserved it or not. All that mattered was that someone else had publicly honored me.

People honor you not because you ask them, but because of the lifestyle you live. With honor comes integrity of character. When you walk in integrity you don't have to go up to someone and say, "Please honor me." They will do it because your character exhibits and demands the utmost respect and honor. When people talk about you or even think about you, whether you are present or not, they will do so with the highest esteem and respect.

You cannot walk in integrity if you are a person who lies, cheats, steals, gambles, uses drugs, abuses others, does not keep your word, etc. Integrity breeds an honest, just, non-judgmental, and loving character. Character is doing the right thing regardless of who may be watching you. Because all that you do, you do to please your audience of One.

Integrity is the main ingredient that enables you to manage your affairs. In managing your affairs with integrity, you alleviate a lot of problems for yourself. Integrity is the foundation for moving from resolution to execution. It is honoring the commitment you made to yourself that prevents you from not faltering.

If you cannot honor the commitments you make to yourself, such as your resolutions, how do you expect to honor the commitments you make to others? Keeping your word to yourself and your resolutions, is imperative to your success in overcoming the barriers that prevent you from fulfilling your commitments. You have to exercise prudence in making vows that you have no intention of keeping. You may say that your goal was to keep them, but I beg to differ, when you do not have a plan of action nor are you willing to do what it takes to be successful. You have failed before you even started.

I used to be very careless about where I parked my car. It didn't matter that almost every single day I got a ticket I knew I had no intention of paying. When they cracked down on those who had been evading paying their tickets, I wanted to blame the system. It wasn't the system that didn't work, it was me. I lacked integrity by not paying for the tickets I received knowing full well that I was disobeying the law.

It is the same when paying any of our obligations. I felt the court system was inconveniencing me by having me go to court for those tickets that were too numerous to count. Yes, they forced me to pay the bulk of them. How dare they!

Along the way, I came to realize that if I parked in a safe place where I would not get a ticket or if I just put the money in the meter, I could avoid having to pay a huge sum of money for penalties. I had a conversation with someone in the same situation and they blamed the fact that where they lived there was no place to park. Didn't they know that when they moved there? They had a responsibility to identify a place where they could park their car without getting tickets and because they elected otherwise, they like me, had to pay for their decision. However, they never took ownership for the decision they made to not locate a secure place to park or to pay the tickets when they had received them.

Managing your affairs takes discipline because you must ask yourself if you should spend money on frivolity when you know that there is a bill to be paid. Rather than take care of your responsibilities, you decide that you want that new outfit. When the bill becomes due you get upset with the creditors because they are asking for the money you promised to pay but didn't because you satisfied a carnal want. It was not a need, but an unadulterated want. If you don't know the difference between a need and a want, you will always satisfy the want on the pretense that it is a need. You need shelter, clothing (not in excess), food and water, but much of the stuff we purchase is more of a want than a need. There is no amount of justification or rationalization because you spent the money to keep a roof over your head, for a new outfit or some other frivolous desire.

We don't always use prudence in our decisions until after the fact. Then it is too late. Hindsight is always better than foresight. Foresightedness is normally a lurking presence tapping you on the shoulder telling you to do what is right, but you elected not to heed its warnings. Hindsight does not warn, it only brings regret.

There is no difference when it comes to paying tithes and saving money. We make the commitment to ourselves that we are going to give God his share and give ourselves a share as well. For some reason, in many instances, God never really gets his share. The integrity of our commitment to God is demonstrated by our actions in fulfilling his commandments and decrees.

Integrity is something you do when no one is watching, at least no one but God and you. In the grand scheme of things, many don't care that He is watching. I think it has something to do with the fact they can't really see Him. I am astonished when people refrain from doing something in front of you, but do it anyway in front of God as though he can't see them. Integrity is transparent regardless of who may be watching.

Resolutions are not kept because of integrity issues. Savings do not increase because of an integrity issue. A healthy lifestyle is not embraced because of an integrity issue. Non-commitment to your own vows or resolutions is an integrity issue. When you are not committed to your own vows, it is hard to be committed to others as well.

At some point, you have to release all those bad habits that have prevented you from walking in your own integrity. Why hold on to them? They have not brought you anywhere near fulfilling your goals. The primary way to release them is to respect the vows that you have made to yourself and do them. In the process of completing them, you will experience success in every area. The more successful you are it will bolster your confidence and you will establish a legacy of success. One success breeds another.

You have to abandon self-sabotaging and self-depleting habits that will keep you from succeeding. This is only accomplished when you are willing to be honest with yourself and introspectively look inward for the answers. If you find yourself in the same situation time and time again, you need to analyze your behavior and realize your culpability in causing it to happen. It almost always echoes of an integrity issue.

Wealth and riches can never be obtained until you are willing to transform your mind-set about your own integrity. Until then, it will elude you and the struggle will always be evident. Amassing wealth means you have to be committed to saving, investing and hard work as well as being diligent in your efforts. Diligence coupled with integrity is an ingredient for success. The more you fulfill your obligations, nothing can stop you from accomplishing everything you set out to accomplish. The habits you incorporate into your daily regimen will determine your success. With each achievement, it puts you that much closer to your goal. Success is in your daily routine. Doing what you need to do every day, will become an integral part of your success. Just watch and see.

Are you willing to do what is necessary to reach your goals? Yes, that means taking off that pretty outfit and putting on some overalls—in essence it is hard work. Whatever commitments you have made it is going to take you being committed to working hard. You must go the extra mile. When you feel like giving up you must force yourself to keep going. You must push yourself.

Your resolutions can only be completed when your dedication to completing them is inherent in the effort you put forth. If there is no effort, there is no commitment. Being dedicated to your efforts in fulfillment of your resolutions, exemplifies not only to you but to everyone that you are a person who keeps their word. Integrity is steeped in honesty of character. That honesty begins with you and extends out to others. Dishonesty with oneself, is dishonesty with others and with God.

Once you realize your resolutions are vows that you not only make to yourself, but you make these vows to God, your commitment to fulfilling them will increase. You pray over them and ask Him for direction and guidance. In essence, you present them to God with a vow to fulfill them. You don't just renege on them to yourself, but you renege to not accomplishing them to God as well. You made a solemn promise to God to do whatever you have vowed to do and elicited His participation in the process. You have asked Him to give you the ability to succeed, yet you don't.

Integrity speaks to your faith in God. Believing that God has given you the ability to fulfill your obligations will cause you to be more diligent in doing them. When you don't, you are essentially saying that you don't believe that God has enabled you to succeed. It also echoes of you depending on yourself, when You should be depending on God. Depending on God in no way releases you from your commitment to fulfilling the vow. Your "yes" must be "Yes" and your "no" must be "No". Therefore, your faith fortifies you to move beyond the limitations of your abilities and to embrace the unlimited ability of God's presence inherent in the power that is inside of you.

Oftentimes you cannot fulfill the vows within your own might, but the Spirit of God living inside of you empowers you to be able to accomplish those things you thought you could not accomplish.

In many instances, that power is not called upon because of lack of faith. As your faith increases, your ability to do what God has called for you to do increases as well. You begin to realize that you cannot do it by yourself. There are times when the task appears to be quite daunting and overwhelming. Rather than do nothing, begin by seeking God for guidance on how to complete it. Not only will the instructions come to you, but when you tackle the thing that you felt you could not accomplish it will be done almost effortlessly without fear. You exercised your faith by seeking God's direction and by acting on those directions. Obedience drives your integrity to experience illimitable success.

Integrity is mind over matter. Every thought must be sprinkled with the integrity of God. "I'd say you'll do best by filling your minds and meditating on things true, noble, reputable, authentic, compelling, gracious—the best, not the worst; the beautiful, not the ugly; things to praise, not things to curse. Put into practice what you learned from me, what you heard and saw and realized. Do that, and God, who makes everything work together, will work you into his most excellent harmonies." Philippians 4.8-9 (Peterson 2002). The transparency of fulfilling your resolutions is that you make the decision to walk in your integrity by doing the right thing even when no one is watching, but you and God. Your commitment to what you say, what you do and how you live synergistically propels you from resolution to execution.

INTROSPECTIVE REFLECTIONS

If we asked people who know you about your integrity what would they say?

_____

_____

_____

What would you say? What would God say?

_____

_____

_____

What areas do you need to improve exercising integrity?

_____

_____

_____

PURPOSEFUL MEDITATIONS

"But as for me, I will walk in mine integrity: redeem me, and be merciful unto me." Psalm 26:11 (King James Version).

"Finally, brethren, whatsoever things are true, whatsoever things are honest, whatsoever things are just, whatsoever things are pure, whatsoever things are lovely, whatsoever things are of good report; if there be any virtue, and if there be any praise, think on these things."
Philippians 4:8 (King James Version).

"He who walks in integrity walks securely, But he who perverts his ways will be found out."
Proverbs 10:9 (New American Standard Bible).

"No one will question your integrity if your integrity is not questionable." Nathanial Bronner Jr. (ThinkExist.com).

"I know, my God, that you test the heart and are pleased with integrity. All these things I have given willingly and with honest intent. And now I have seen with joy how willingly your people who are here have given to you."
1 Chronicles 29:17 (New International Version).

"A good man sheweth favour, and lendeth: he will guide his affairs with discretion." Psalm 112:5 (King James Version).

PRAYER OF DECISION

Father, Help me to walk circumspectly regardless of who sees me or not because Your eyes are always on me. Deliver me of anything that prevents me from exhibiting a lifestyle of integrity that does not reflect You. Bless me to do the right thing always. Whatever I do, I will do with the utmost integrity as I glorify and honor You as a marketplace influencer.
Amen.

NOTES

I DECIDED

chapter five
DISCIPLINE
Can I? Or Can't I?

f it feels good–do it! At some point, we have all uttered those words. If you've never said them, know that your actions echoed them loud and clear. How many times have you done something you knew you should not do, yet you did it anyway? You then had to suffer the consequences or truths for your actions.

We all fall prey to this when it comes to shopping (especially women). We see something and convince ourselves that we just have to have it. We rationalize why we should buy it and we persuade ourselves we absolutely need that new pair of red shoes. It doesn't matter that we already have ten pairs! Yet we walk out that store and take them home. For days a small voice whispers to us, "You don't really need these shoes. Return them." The coveted possession almost never gets returned, because the carnality of our want supersedes the truth of our need.

Helping a friend move personified this preoccupation with behavior that was out of control. More than a third of her clothes, and there were many, still had the tags on them. They had never been worn. Never! Not to mention shoes of the same style in different colors–and in some instances of the same color. Overindulgent behavior exemplifies a lack of discipline.

When it comes to most things, we operate in the same self-indulgence. We overindulge knowing we should exercise self-control. Although something may be all right for you to do, it doesn't necessarily mean it is the best thing for you to do. All of us must eat, but we don't have to overeat to the point of gluttony wondering why we are not losing weight. God created intimacy for marriage, but we don't have to fornicate or commit adultery. I had a friend who once said she knew God was going to understand that she just had to have sex, as though this justified her lack of self-control and her commitment to fornication.

Rationalizing your behavior in justification of you doing what you want to do, does not negate the fact that you have a responsibility to do the right thing. Until you stop justifying your undisciplined behavior, you will never establish a disciplined lifestyle.

Self-control always precedes a decision. God has given us free will to make choices. However, he also proscribed in His Word the right choices we should make. God did not allow Solomon, the wisest man to ever live, to provide us with hundreds of prosperous living proverbs if He didn't expect us to follow them. God knew we would be drawn to the pleasures of this world; however, He also tells us that none of these pleasures should control or consume us.

Unbridled negative behavior prevents you from moving from resolution to execution. It robs you of all God has for you. Lack of discipline causes you to miss God's blessing. Overindulgent desires skew reasoning and forces you into the wilderness.

These self-imposed wilderness experiences could be avoided if discipline were exercised.

It takes a great deal of self-control to do what you are supposed to do when you are supposed to do it. One of the greatest enemies is a lack of self-control. To achieve goals, no matter what they may be, you must discipline yourself.

It takes discipline to stop smoking when you have become accustomed to it. One of my sisters has suffered a few heart attacks. During one of her times of recovery, I asked the doctor about her smoking habit. We discussed with the doctor her rationalizing how she felt certain foods contributed to her heart problems. The doctor emphatically stated that he couldn't say for certain if eating specific types of foods had something to do with it, but he knew for certain that her cigarette smoking was a major contributor. Although she has meticulously eliminated certain foods from her diet, smoking cigarettes continue to be one of her greatest pleasures and she refuses to give them up. As she puts it, "You're going to die from something anyway."

To achieve your goals, no matter what it is, you must discipline yourself. If you want to lose weight, you must discipline yourself to eat healthily. If you want to exercise, again you must carve out the time and make sure you do it. If you want more intimacy with God, you must set aside time with Him. It's a blessing to know that in our quest to exercise self-control we can lean on God for strength and know He will not suffer us to endure more than we can bear.

If you want to break a bad habit, it takes self-control to not indulge in the activity. If you want to establish a good habit, it takes discipline to make a point of doing it consistently. Discipline attached to any goal ensures your success. Yes, you must be committed to discipline—or should I say submitted to discipline.

There is a certain amount of submission that takes place in disciplining yourself to reach your desired outcome.

Whatever you submit to, you give it the authority to help you withstand whatever you are facing or trying to conquer. The more you submit to it, the more successful you are in overcoming that which seeks to overcome you. Submitting yourself to a disciplined lifestyle ensures that every resolution you make you will be able to achieve. Whatever obstacles there may be trying to prevent your success, you will be able to overcome them because you have submitted yourself to be disciplined.

My success was inherent in prayer, fasting and consecrating my resolutions and myself. For many people disciplining one's self to establish a prayer life augmented with fasting is something they don't want to do. I say don't want to do because this too is a choice. It becomes of paramount importance if you truly want to be successful, you have to bring yourself under submission to prayer and fasting. As I said, whatever you submit yourself to will enable you to overcome the thing that seeks to overcome you. There is nothing to increase your ability to withstand attacks and undisciplined behavior than prayer and fasting.

It is in the intimacy of prayer that God begins to reveal you to you. Even more importantly, during this time He begins to reveal His purpose for you. He doesn't just reveal His purpose for you, but the discipline of prayer and fasting will fortify you to fulfill that purpose. Steeped in every resolution is the purpose God has for your life that is actually connected to the very essence of your existence. Along the way, life prevents you from achieving them. You seek a higher power within yourself to be successful. That takes prayer and fasting.

Don't abhor the daily regimen of prayer coupled with the harnessing power of fasting to enable you to reach your goals. Both are imperative. They teach you how to take control over what you perceive to be uncontrollable. Seek God about when to fast, how to fast and how long to fast. He will bring clarity to you through His Holy Spirit. Pray and ask God for His strength to enable you to embrace fasting and to be successful.

I am not going to tell you that it is easy. If it was easy, would it be worth it? Whatever is worth fighting for is not going to be easy, but believe me, it is worth it. You fight for discipline. Within the constraints of discipline, you will achieve illimitable success. Disciplining yourself to achieve what God envisioned for you is more than worth the sacrifice. Oftentimes success eludes us because we are not willing to gird up our insatiable appetites to overcome short-lived pleasure.

Insatiable behavior is indicative of self-centeredness and selfishness. Selfishness is at the core of every extra-marital affair. The person does not consider the ramifications from their actions, because what is important is for them to satisfy that carnal need even at the expense of their family's needs. Some may say that as long as the family is not aware, then it is fine. But that is not true. There is a certain amount of thievery from undisciplined selfish behavior. Every moment the person spends indulging in the affair they are taking valuable time away from their spouse and children. Whatever money they spend, they are taking money from their household to support the affair. Everything they do they rob their family of that luxury, and they give it to someone else with the primary focus on satisfying themselves. Not only does it take away from their family, but it robs them of fulfilling their own obligations to themselves. The time spent in the affair, can be valuable time spent accomplishing their personal, professional and spiritual goals.

Why is it some people achieve success and some people don't? It has to do with discipline. It takes a lot of strength to say no to the pleasures of life. Our society is bombarded with one pleasure after another to lure you away from doing what you need to do. It is easy to be distracted. Sometimes the allure of everyday living is a major culprit—especially against perceived responsibilities that are rooted in guilt-laden obligations.

Part of being successful in fulfilling your goals is having a plan of action. When you don't have a plan of action every day, someone will lure you into their plan. Family members are especially notorious for this. Their emergency becomes your emergency even if it is not an actual emergency. Somehow, they make it a familial obligation while pulling at your heartstrings of compassion and before you know it your well-made plans are altered. What you set out to accomplish you are not able to accomplish. That is not to say there are no true family emergencies that do occur, there are. You have to evaluate the situation as to whether it is an emergency for you to stop whatever you are doing and to be caught up into someone else's perceived emergency.

Disciplining yourself to say no without guilt is required. If not, you will never get anything done. People will constantly call you into their situations regardless of what your plans may be. The "no" becomes a powerful weapon in maintaining your focus.

That same "no" must be exercised against yourself as well. You must learn how to say no to those things that are not in your best interest. No one can coerce you to do something that you don't want to do. Your confidence to refrain from those negative behaviors or doing what you don't want to do begins with discipline. Your success is your ability to walk away and your ability to do the right thing. Making a daily decision to do what you know you should be doing can be mastered if you want to master it.

Inherent in the Spirit of God is the ability to exercise self-control over self-indulgent behavior.

I realized that moving from resolution to execution I had to tap into the power within me—the Holy Spirit to lead and guide me. I knew that within the finiteness of who I am I could not do it myself. I had tried for many years and it was obvious I was not being successful. God has given us the power of His Spirit to be overcomers. The Holy Spirit provides us the ability not to be under the control of anything. The more knowledge I acquired about the Holy Spirit and embraced Him to lead and guide me, I found myself accomplishing my resolutions and experiencing success. The Holy Spirit became my friend, that is always with me and whom I can call on at a moment's notice.

According to 1 Corinthians 10:23 (King James Version), all things are lawful, but that doesn't mean that all things are expedient. God created food for us to eat, but he never meant for food to become a controlling force in our lives. Overindulgence in your eating habits is like connecting yourself to the harlotry of this world. It is not being respectful of the Holy Spirit that dwells inside of you. For that matter, anything that you overindulge in doing is being disrespectful to the Holy Spirit. You are saying that the Spirit of God inside of you is not more powerful than your insatiable appetite for the carnality of this world.

You may be disciplined in one area and not in another. Discipline is a learned behavior that you can garner from those areas where you have mastered it. Everyone battles against our own will. We know what we should be doing, but we don't always do it. There is a battle of the wills that is waged inside of us daily. Disciplined behavior enables you to win that battle when You allow the Holy Spirit to lead and guide you.

We want to be successful and become everything God envisioned, but we must adopt discipline into our lives. You must be able to discern what you need to be doing and to do it. Every single day you have to be disciplined enough to review your goals and to do something toward them. If not, you will never experience the success God envisioned for you.

Success is in our daily routine because frequency breeds acceptance. The more you do it, the more it becomes a part of you. Every successful person got there not by mere intelligence, but through discipline and due diligence. Exercising temperance is a virtue to not only be celebrated, but to be coveted and to fight for it every day. One thing is for sure, when you exercise self-control, you immediately reap its rewards and your resolution becomes a reality because you are dedicated to exercising daily discipline to execute them every single day.

INTROSPECTIVE REFLECTIONS

Are you out of control?

_____

_____

_____

Do you make a practice of overindulgence?

_____

_____

_____

Do you allow bad habits to conquer you rather than you conquer them?

_____

_____

_____

What are you going to do about it?

_____

_____

_____

PURPOSEFUL MEDITATIONS

*"I do not do the good things I want to do, but I do the
bad things I do not want to do. So, if I do things I do not want
to do, then I am not the one doing them. It is sin living in me
that does those things. So, I have learned this rule: When I want
to do good, evil is there with me. In my mind, I am happy with
God's law."* Romans 7:19-22 (New Century Version).

*"But I need something more! For if I know the law but
still can't keep it, and if the power of sin within me keeps
sabotaging my best intentions, I obviously need help!
I realize that I don't have what it takes. I can will it, but I can't
do it. I decide to do good, but I don't really do it; I decide not
to do bad, but then I do it anyway. My decisions, such as they
are, don't result in actions. Something has gone wrong deep
within me and gets the better of me every time. It happens so
regularly that it's predictable. The moment I decide to
do good, sin is there to trip me up. I truly delight in God's
commands, but it's pretty obvious that not all of me joins
in that delight. Parts of me covertly rebel, and just when
I least expect it, they take charge."*
Romans 7:17-23 (Peterson 2002).

"It's not the work that's hard, it's the discipline." Anonymous.

*"The night is far spent, the day is at hand: let us therefore
cast off the works of darkness, and let us put on the armour
of light. Let us walk honestly, as in the day; not in rioting and*

drunkenness, not in chambering and wantonness, not in strife and envying. But put ye on the Lord Jesus Christ, and make not provision for the flesh, to fulfil the lusts thereof."
Romans 13:13-14, (King James Version).

"And we are instructed to turn from Godless living and sinful pleasures. We should live in this evil world with self-control, right conduct, and devotion to God."
Titus 2:12, (The Living Bible).

"If it is to be, it is up to me." Anonymous.

Prayer of Decision

Father, There is so much temptation confronting me and sometimes I have a hard time walking away and doing the right thing. Please help me to exercise self-control in making wise choices and adhering to the plan that has been set forth. Teach me how not to indulge in activities that are not expedient for my well-being and only come to distract me from fulfilling my goals and living the dreams and desires you placed inside of me.
Amen.

NOTES

NOTES

_____

_____

_____

_____

_____

_____

_____

_____

_____

_____

_____

_____

_____

_____

_____

_____

_____

_____

_____

_____

_____

_____

_____

_____

_____

_____

_____

_____

_____

chapter six
ENTHUSIASM
Enthusiasm Heals the Soul

Several years ago, I met a student who attended Howard University. At the time I was unemployed. The thing that impressed her most was that I was so happy. She told her friends she met a woman who was the happiest person she ever met, even though she didn't have a job! She kept saying that she would be out of her mind if she didn't have a job. She and I still chuckle about her reaction.

The vicissitudes of life happen—some good and some bad. How we approach them have more to do with our attitude than anything else. When you begin to embrace enthusiasm, you don't allow circumstances or people to adversely affect your joy. Allowing outside forces to adversely affect your emotions, causes you to relinquish control of your joy to someone else. The vicissitudes of life will always impact us, but you decide to be joyful no matter what your choice may be.

The hindsight of life enables us to realize that the trials and tribulations we endured were more critical to our growth than the triumphs. God instructs us not to embrace joy in hindsight of the persecution, but to do so in the midst of it. While it may appear difficult to maintain your joy during adversity, if you hold on to it when you get to the other side you are a stronger and better person. Joy is the wellspring of your soul. Even in the face of adversity, you can remain enthusiastic because of the joy inherent inside of you. Joy is beyond a happy moment or an exhilarating feeling, it is a mind-set and a place of being that provides you with the strength to withstand the harshest of life's circumstances.

You may experience some setbacks and you may receive some disconcerting news, but you will not lose your joy. You may cry about losing a loved one, but you won't be so consumed with the grief that you lose sight of your joy. It is enthusiasm laden with passion that enables you to keep forging forward when it appears all odds are against you succeeding. You simply refuse to allow circumstances to control your feelings, actions or outcomes.

People look for the semblance of joy in so many places—drugs, alcohol, sex, gambling and anything that brings a temporary fix through a synthetic substitute. One day while driving past a bar I noticed the sign on the outside stating that spirits were sold there. After that day I started noticing that many bars or clubs had that same declaration. People flock to the bars seeking to find joy inherent in the artificial spirit inside of a beer, wine or liquor bottle. It is deceptive because it leads one to believe that the satisfaction of joy they seek can be found in a bottle. Yet, the spirit that they latch on to is not to bring them joy, but to start them down a spiral path of gloom and doom. In essence, it is a counterfeit to the real joy inherent in the Spirit of God.

Many are caroused into disillusionment because they believe the hype of the synthetic perceived joy givers such as drugs, alcohol, sex, gambling and more. Once lured down these destructive paths one finds themselves unable to live out the destiny of their lives. It doesn't matter who you are or your socio-economic status, these are things that will take you off course. These are the things that cause you not to fulfill your vows. Don't be disillusioned with the promises of their abilities to bring lasting joy, they do not have the power to do that. It is a temporary fix that has no lasting value and ultimately causes more problems than they solve.

The joy that spurs you onward to fulfilling your goals is not temporary. Without it, you won't be able to be as successful as you would be with it. Along the way, you are going to encounter some challenges. It is an attitude of fortitude that gives you the resiliency to bounce back, overcome difficulties and bypass temptations.

Everyone needs motivation. There comes a time when you are not going to feel like doing what you know you should do. Believe me, there will be those days when it seems like you can't pull yourself from the bed. How do you muster the strength to get up when it appears there is nothing to get up for? Your excitement for the assignment is what is going to keep you from wasting days away doing nothing. Every day the abundance of joy is what will motivate you to keep moving forward in achieving your goals.

A merry heart is medicine to the soul. It has been documented that many deathly-ill people were able to overcome life-threatening sickness and disease because of their enthusiastic attitudes toward the illness and life. It is no different for you. Transform your attitude and you can transform the trajectory of your destiny and your life.

Laughter does good, like medicine. Laugh at life. Laugh at your mistakes and keep it moving. Learn to laugh and to feel the laughter overflowing from the depths of your soul. Allow it to gush forth like a wellspring of living water, because it is truly living water for your very existence. If you can't laugh at yourself, who can? It forces you to put things in perspective and not be consumed with worry and anxiety. Worry and anxiety will not get you anywhere. I do mean that literally. While you are worrying and fretting, you could be doing something toward accomplishing your goals.

If you feel that you can't get yourself out of the doldrums, do something that can. Take a small break and find someone or something that makes you laugh. My mother used to store up funny jokes to laugh at a later time. I will sometimes just turn on the television and watch a sitcom that makes me laugh. There is something about the endorphins that are released when you laugh that causes your outlook to become more positive. When your outlook is positive you stay on course to completing your resolutions.

The inner confidence joy brings is immeasurable. It makes the difference in your perspective and your attitude. Joy also is one of the major ingredients leading you down a successful path. Even in adversity, you will always be able to see the rainbow, the promises of God that the best is yet to come. Hold on to them as you become all He created you to be. His promises bring hope and hope brings joy.

A celebrated radio personality in Detroit used to proclaim every day, "I refuse to be unhappy today!" I adopted that proclamation. Your joy strengthens you to endure the hardships of life with optimism in the same fashion you do your triumphs. Life is going to happen. Life is happening every day. Things are going to happen beyond your control. Stop blaming yourself. Stop having a "woe is me" moment and move forward. It's when you get stuck in the pitfalls of life that you lose your joy. When you lose your joy, you lose your ability to do what you need to do. When you lose your ability to do what you need to do, you simply give up. Always remember you are maneuvering through it and never getting stuck in it.

As you move from resolution to execution you no longer allow life to deplete your joy. You learn how to truly count it all joy because you realize that God is doing something special in you as He perfects you to achieve great things. Your circumstances do not determine your joy, but your determination to be joyful does have a direct bearing on how you react to your circumstances. Enthusiasm is the passion that keeps your fire burning. Never lag in zeal; be aglow and on fire with an abundance of passionate joy that propels you to succeed from a place of resolution to the empowering place of execution.

INTROSPECTIVE REFLECTIONS

What do you allow to steal your joy?

_____

_____

_____

Do you embrace life with joy regardless if it is good, bad or indifferent?

_____

_____

_____

Do you allow outside stimulus to dictate your inner joy?

_____

_____

_____

How can you maintain joyful optimism regardless of your circumstances?

_____

_____

_____

PURPOSEFUL MEDITATIONS

"Go thy way, eat thy bread with joy, and drink thy wine with a merry heart; for God now accepteth thy works." Ecclesiastes 9:7 (King James Version).

"The precepts of the LORD are right, giving joy to the heart. The commands of the LORD are radiant, giving light to the eyes." Psalm 19:8 (New International Version).

"Success is going from failure to failure without loss of enthusiasm." Anonymous.

"This is the day the LORD has made; let us rejoice and be glad in it." Psalm 118:24 (King James Version).

"Rejoice in the Lord always. I will say it again: Rejoice!" Philippians 4:4 (New International Version).

Prayer of Decision

Father, I need your joy that is the wellspring of life. Thank you for your unspeakable joy that lifts my spirits no matter what happens. I may not know what the future holds, and it may seem as though everything is going against me, but I know that as long as you have my future in your hands I will enthusiastically embrace life and walk in unspeakable joy every single day.
Amen.

NOTES

I DECIDED

chapter seven

DEDICATION

Dedication Achieves Success

While having breakfast with a colleague who managed up-and-coming professional golfers, we ran into a young man who expressed a desire to be represented by him. My colleague chatted with him about his desire to become a pro golfer and promised to connect with him at a later date.

Once the man walked away my colleague stated that the man was not serious about becoming a professional golfer. Inquisitively, I inquired why he made that assumption. He went on to say that he was just going out to practice and it was well past ten o'clock in the morning. He stated that those who are serious about their professional golfing careers are the ones whose dedication included being on the golf course early and not finishing until they had given it their all every single day.

Without being dedicated to achieving your goals every day, success will evade you. Hundreds experience dreams deferred because they were not determined to bring those dreams into reality, just like that golfer. What happens to a dream deferred? Absolutely nothing! It lies dormant and never moves from a dream into reality. Ultimately it is taken to the graveyard where so many other dreams lie buried under tombstones.

Fatal distractions were created for one reason and that is to take you off course from your God-given assignment. When you have committed yourself to do something, you also have to be even more committed when the distractions appear. Recognize them for what they are and move forward. Part of that recognition has a lot to do with planning and knowing yourself.

If you have no plan, especially a daily plan of action, when distractions occur they easily pull you away from what you know you should be doing. You must be just as committed to the planning process as you are to the execution of the plan. In essence, resolutions without execution are like having no plan at all.

Many are afraid to dedicate themselves to anything. They meander aimlessly through life with no direction or purpose. When you become committed to something you begin to gain a better sense as to who you are and who God created you to be. For instance, when you commit yourself to Christ, you no longer have to wonder about your destiny and purpose after the cessation of this life. You begin to have a clearer perspective as to who you are and why you were created.

With any commitment comes responsibility. You cannot be committed to something and neglect the very thing you claim to be committed to. You can't become discouraged when it appears things are not as large as you envisioned. For your dreams to manifest you must be dedicated to achieving them each day, regardless of the magnitude of your perception of the dream. Oftentimes your perception is what is hindering you from getting up and doing what is necessary. You perceive the assignment to be much larger than what it really is and you create a false sense of being overwhelmed by a task that is not overwhelming. Once you commit to doing it and find yourself in the midst of doing it, your hindsight bias provides you with the reality of the task. What appeared to overwhelm you, no longer frightens you. You have taken control over it by taking the first step by starting it.

Dedication to the start is the first hurdle of any resolution. The start has its own nuances of fear and anxiety. From the onset, you can feel that you are defeated before you even start because you don't know how to begin. Feeling as though you don't know where to start can keep you from starting. You cannot allow yourself to become so consumed with the beginning that you never do anything. I want to share a secret with you in your commitment to get moving. Just do it. You have to determine within your own resolve that you are going to do just what you have committed to do even as fear stares you down. Know that you are much more powerful than the fear when you step out and begin to tackle the thing that wants you to believe it has tackled you. Nothing can take control over your destiny unless you relinquish control to it.

You must learn how to celebrate the small beginnings. You alone are the only one who can prevent the distractions of life to keep you from moving forward.

Yes, there will be distractions. How you react to the distractions will make the difference to your success. Dedication entails sacrificing things you may want to do to realize your dreams. There are going to be innumerable activities and social events that you may want to attend, but you will have to evaluate how important they are to you. Or, more importantly, how important are they over you doing what is necessary to be successful? This is a hard place because there is a huge part of you who wants to be with family and friends. Yet, within your heart-of-hearts, you know that you can't. Or, you can. If you do, it may set you back from achieving your goal.

You have to muster up the determination within yourself to refrain from doing things that take you away from your assignment. You see with every resolution there is always an assignment attached to it. How important the assignment is to you and your commitment to fulfilling that assignment will determine your success. If you haphazardly commit to it, then you will haphazardly approach it and never achieve your desired outcome of success. In essence, you will either half do it or you won't do it at all. A half-hearted commitment to anything, results in a half-hearted effort and half-hearted success.

Jesus was committed to providing a better way for people. As a result, He sacrificed his own life, so we could be free and inherit eternal life and experience abundant life on earth. You have to be determined that there is absolutely nothing that will stop you from doing what you need to do. There will always be things that you want to do and you just won't be able to do them, that is, if you are serious. Sometimes it is hard to recognize those subtle distractions because they may appear to be what you should be doing, and they are not. When you develop a plan of action and adhere to that plan you can circumvent those deceptive mimicking distractions that try to take you away from what you need to be doing.

There is nothing wrong with resolutions, but the problem happens when you are not dedicated and determined to move them from being mere words on paper to make them a reality in your life. The resolutions should help guide you forward as you do the corresponding actions that lead to your success.

INTROSPECTIVE REFLECTIONS

Do you make a commitment to yourself and don't keep it?

_____

_____

_____

Are you dedicated to doing what you need to do every single day?

_____

_____

_____

Do you manage distractions, or do you allow distractions to manage you?

_____

_____

_____

PURPOSEFUL MEDITATIONS

"Being confident of this very thing, that he which hath begun a good work in you will perform it until the day of Jesus Christ." Philippians 1:6 (King James Version).

"I beseech you therefore, brethren, by the mercies of God, that ye present your bodies a living sacrifice, holy, acceptable unto God, which is your reasonable service. And be not conformed to this world: but be ye transformed by the renewing of your mind, that ye may prove what is that good, and acceptable, and perfect, will of God." Romans (King James Version).

*"We all have dreams. But in order to make dreams
come into reality, it takes an awful lot of determination,
dedication, self-discipline, and effort."*
Jesse Owens (Famous Quotes at BrainyQuote n.d.).

*"Let us hold fast the profession of our faith
without wavering; (for he is faithful that promised)."*
Hebrews 10:23 (King James Version).

*"True strength lies in submission which permits one to dedicate
his life, through devotion, to something beyond himself."*
Henry Miller (Famous Quotes at BrainyQuote n.d.).

*"The person who makes a success of living is the one
who sees his goal steadily and aims for it unswervingly.
That is dedication."* Cecil B. De Mille (Attitudes.com 2018).

*"I learned patience, perseverance, and dedication. Now
I really know myself, and I know my voice. It's a voice of
pain and victory."* Anthony Hamilton
(Famous Quotes at BrainyQuote n.d.).

PRAYER OF DECISION

*Father, Bless me to be dedicated to become all you created
me to be, because the plans you have for me is for a bright
future with endless possibilities. Every day as I become more
dedicated to living my dreams and fulfilling my purpose,
I will seek you and know I will find you. Not only will I find
You, I will discover who you created me to be. It is in this
self-discovery that my understanding will be expanded
to reinforce my dedication to my destiny, fulfilling my
purpose and achieving illimitable success.
Amen.*

NOTES

NOTES

_____

_____

_____

_____

_____

_____

_____

_____

_____

_____

_____

_____

_____

_____

_____

_____

_____

_____

_____

_____

_____

_____

_____

_____

_____

_____

_____

_____

_____

_____

chapter eight

GOALS WITHIN THE GOAL

A Blueprint For Success

H ave you ever given much thought about Creation and the lessons God has given us? One thing for sure, God could have instantly created into existence the entire world and the universe with stars, animals, fish of the sea, light and darkness, and even humankind. Yet God took six days to do what he could have done in an instant. God already knew the plan. He just needed His plan to unfold.

Everything is a process. First, you must be able to conceive it. God gives us a vision and provides a glimpse into what our destiny and purpose will be. Just like when He looked over the Earth and saw a vastness of darkness and emptiness. In actuality, He saw potential.

God begins with darkness and emptiness in each of us. There is a void that exists, and we wander aimlessly until we are able to connect with the light. Once we embrace the light God immediately proclaimed, "Let there be light." Instantaneously, the sea of darkness and emptiness is transformed into the light. Just like Creation.

God impregnates us, and we don't always see the seed because of the darkness. In the moment when we can perceive the vision, things come into focus. This is the beginning of the beginning.

Every day God worked His plan. Each day He knew at the close of the day He should have accomplished what He set out to accomplish for that day. At the cessation of the day, He would have achieved His goals. Each day built on the accomplishments of the previous day.

In essence, God took each day and separated each task into sub-tasks. This enabled Him to accomplish what He needed to accomplish for that respective day. He created time and separated it into seven days with the goal of achieving His plan for that day. Every day He assigned that day with tasks that had to be accomplished on that day.

At the cessation of each day, God took a moment to assess His accomplishments and saw that it was good. You must include reflective moments for assessment that propels you forward.

Every day God planned His day. Once His day was planned He worked the plan. At the end of each day, He knew that he had completed every task assigned to that day. Each day He saw the vision of the world and universe take shape. At the end of the sixth day, all that He had set out to do was done.

God demonstrated that we have the same authority to command our day as He did. God, who is the author and finisher of our faith, combined the super with the natural and provided us with a blueprint for success. That blueprint illustrates that every day you need to plan; even if you must force yourself to adopt this discipline and incorporate into your life. Rest must be an integral part for you to recuperate, be renewed and refreshed, so you can take authority over your planning success.

Conceive the vision. Work the vision. Every day take authority over the vision with planning. God has given us a vision to run with it. Over the course of your life, God expects you to embrace the vision so you can truly achieve and fulfill your purpose as you maximize your time wisely.

I still marvel at such a well-oiled machine to fulfill the mandate of the United States Decennial Census that is conducted every 10 years. It revs up and increases it's intensity as it nears the official Census Day. There are unmovable deadlines and countless activities to ensure everyone in America and its properties are counted by the April deadline. I was privileged to be a part of this amazing countdown during the 2010 United States Decennial Census.

We had no choice but to meet each deadline because they were set in stone. We unequivocally knew that when December hit, everything had to be submitted to President Barack Obama. Everyone feverishly scurried around using every talent and ability they had to make things happen before that fateful date. Before one Census ends, the government is already revving up for the next one.

It reminds me of a New Year. As we approach the finality of one year we arbitrarily place deadlines on ourselves and develop a list of resolutions and goals we plan to attain in the ensuing year. Just like we were in a countdown for the Census, each of us experiences a countdown to accomplish all God has placed inside of us.

For instance, if you envision how much time you have from the first day of the year to the last, you would probably do more with your gift of time. Every year each of us is granted 365 days to use prudently and at our own discretion. Now, when you realize that these 365 days breakdown into 8,760 hours, 525,600 minutes and 31,536,000 seconds, you realize what a priceless gift we have been given. *How awesome is that!*

God tells us to number our days, so we can apply our hearts to wisdom. Each of us has been given a finite amount of time in our lifetime. We are to maximize each moment prudently. Every year He bestows upon us the opportunity to fulfill our purpose while making a difference in someone else's life. Just like with the Census, the time is going to pass, and December will no longer loom on the horizon, it will be upon you.

The question looms, "What are you going to do with this priceless gift?"

This marks the first day of your beginning. It may be at the beginning of the calendar year or another date, but it is the beginning. You still have a huge blank canvas of seconds, minutes, hours and days that loom before you. Do you sit aimlessly day in and day out revisiting those goals that you never seem to accomplish? Or, do you put forth a concerted effort to maximize your gift by doing something every day to ensure that when December, or your designated goal date hits, you have done all you could to fulfill your desires and dreams. In the process, helped someone else achieve theirs.

The beauty of this gift is that no one can take it from you. Oh, but yes, you can squander it away. Whether you use the time or not it will be gone forever. The choice is yours. When my nephew was critically ill, his wife's co-workers gave her their personal sick time, so she would be able to be with him. That is not the case when it comes to our real lives. It cannot be re-gifted and no one else can give you some of their time to replace yours. Once it is gone, it is gone. The time is going to pass regardless. Now, what you do and how you use it becomes paramount. It is up to you because the countdown has already begun. Day one…day two…day three….

PRIORITY IS NUMBER ONE

Prioritizing our lives is extremely important. No matter how much we plan, we always need to make room for contingencies. Yet, we must learn to prioritize. If we don't we meander through life without a clear direction of our purpose or where we are going.

When you begin to prioritize your life, you have to realize that the best-laid plans sometimes can be altered. Sometimes circumstances beyond our control can cause our plans to go out the window. Had no priority been set, we would have been still trying to fulfill obligations when it was evident they no longer were the priority.

Yet, we must establish priorities to be successful. There are times when you may not be able to fulfill all your goals. However, if you don't establish a hierarchy of order for your goals you probably won't accomplish any of them.

If you don't prioritize, you will find yourself pulled in many directions, and never able to complete anything. Prioritization prevents you from being distracted. Yes, distractions exist because other people feel they also have a right to your time. And they will if you permit them to invade your time and your space.

Establishing clearly delineated priorities empowers you to inform others that you can't talk with them or hang out with them. In essence, your agenda is your responsibility. It is not theirs. Conversely, their agenda is theirs. It is not yours. Keep this in mind when you feel guilty for telling someone you have to complete an assignment and can't talk or meet them during that specific time. If not, you will never reach the goals you have established.

Prioritizing means you will be able to do all the things you want to do including spending time with family and friends. If not, you will not be able to accomplish anything. More than just writing your goals down, prioritize them so you can be even more effective regardless of what may happen.

Establishing goals without checks and balances is like setting yourself up for defeat. It is these checks and balances that enable you to ascertain your true commitment and your progress. It forces you to re-examine your deficiencies and institute measures to overcome them. Conversely, it's also a time to celebrate victories and continue with what has been successful. This will move you into a new realm of accountability and responsibility.

Do we have faith? Yes, we do have faith. Faith without works is dead as dead can be. It is meaningless. We might as well not have faith at all. You must marry your faith with works. Faith is an actionable verb...it is fluid. It is forever moving in the natural as much as it is moving in the spiritual. It is dynamic!

"My people are destroyed for lack of knowledge..."
Hosea 4:6 (King James Version).

"Where there is no vision, the people perish..."
Proverbs 29:18 (King James Version)

"Write the vision and make it plain."
Habakkuk 2:2 (King James Version).

SUCCESS BEGINS IN WRITING IT DOWN

Why do you think God instructed you to write your vision? So you can have understanding. That means you must take time to introspectively analyze all aspects of your life as you develop goals with a determination to keep your goals and ultimately to achieve them.

Success is linked to your daily routine and that is where your success in executing your resolutions begins. Regardless of whether you set long-term or short-term goals, achieving those goals will be linked to your commitment to take some action toward them every single day. No action. No success. No victory. Action is the propelling force leading you down a path of unlimited success.

What I'd like for you to do is to take the time and think of some goals you would like to achieve. You don't want to haphazardly come up with goals you have no intention of achieving or that they are way out of your scope or ability to achieve. Be realistic. This is not an exercise of futility where you just throw something on paper for the sake of doing it. You are taking control of your destiny by strategically devising achievable goals that you truly want to achieve. These are not your pipe dreams. These are your dreams that have moved out of the pipes on their way to becoming a reality.

Initially, you are going to focus on writing goals you can achieve in a week. Think about those goals and write them down. This exercise will help to jump-start your goal setting ability. Achieving your first week's goals will bolster your confidence to not only write the goals but to stick to it. This is your launching pad. Remember to find joy in the small beginnings!

Transformation is only successful when taken in small doses. Developing a planning strategy for one week will begin to help you develop strategies for a month, several months, a year, five years and even a lifetime. You see, no matter how much you want change to happen, there is always a starting point. The starting point is what gives you the confidence to move forward and the assurance to know you can do it.

Write realistic achievable goals for the ensuing week in the following areas – spiritual, relational, physical, financial, emotional, environmental, social and professional. Set goals for these areas or only for those areas you feel you will be able to complete within a week.

Below are examples of goals you may use as a guide. You are not limited to these examples, and feel free to create your own. The most important aspects of goal setting are to make them achievable with the unmitigated determination to stick to them. Let's get started!

1. SPIRITUAL – I plan to attend church at least once this week…I plan to go to Bible Study on Tuesday night…I plan to read a passage of Scripture from the Bible each day…I plan to wake up fifteen minutes early and pray.

2. RELATIONAL – I plan to spend more time with my family…I will take my children to the playground…I will establish a date night with my spouse…I want to have a meaningful relationship…I will reach out to my parents, siblings and other close loved ones.

3. PHYSICAL – I plan to exercise at least three times this week…I plan to eat only fruits and vegetables…I plan to drink more water and less carbonated drinks…I will walk three days each week.

4. FINANCIAL – I plan to pay 10 percent tithes off my gross earnings…I plan to save at least 10 percent of my income…I plan to spend my money wisely and not buy anything I really don't need.

5. EMOTIONAL – I plan to be joyful each day …I plan to read motivational and inspirational books to transform my mind-set to be more positive.

6. ENVIRONMENTAL (organized/tidy areas) – I plan to clean out the garage…I plan to get my clothes organized…I plan to clean my car.

7. SOCIAL (cultural - visit a museum, contribute to your community, etc.) – I plan to go to the museum…I plan to use words that build up and not tear down…I plan not to use profanity…I plan to go to a shelter and volunteer my time.

8. PROFESSIONAL (career, job or business) – I plan to start my own business…I plan to arrive at work on time…I plan to meet my deadlines…I plan to seek another position…I plan to mentor others.

Using the example shown below complete the Goal Setting Template by writing down at least one goal in each respective area you feel you can attain in one week's time. Each section of the template needs to be completed, even if it is for one week.

The sections are:

Date: This is the date you write the goal down. Working forward from this date you will begin to identify the goals within the goal and include each incremental step that moves you forward.

Goal: This is the overall goal you want to achieve. Make sure you clearly and exactly define your goal. We have supplied you with some examples of goals, but you are in no way limited to those. Make sure you give thought to your goals and don't just haphazardly write down goals that you know you won't be committed to achieving.

Goal Category: Listed are eight categories to be used in your goal setting. Almost every goal you write will fall within these eight categories, but you are not limited to these. Feel free to explore your own categories as well.

Spiritual–Growing and maturing spiritually.

Relational–Establishing better relationships with spouses, family, friends and others.

Physical–Establishing a healthy lifestyle that includes exercise, eating healthy and getting the necessary rest and sleep.

Financial–Managing money and investments.

Emotional–Maintaining a healthy attitude toward life.

Environmental–Establishing and maintaining organization in your physical surroundings.

Social–Incorporating leisure time to take advantage of social and cultural events.

Professional–Pursuing career, job, business and entrepreneurial quests.

Scripture: You should have a Scripture for each goal. As you strive to fulfill your goals, meditating on Scripture reinforces your commitment and provide you with added strength during moments of weariness.

Steps to Achieve Goals: These are goals within the goal. They are the incremental steps that will help you in fulfilling the ultimate goal. This is important because you must be able to have a measuring yardstick to keep you on your path to success. For each goal within the goal that you complete it will bolster your confidence to complete the overall objective.

Is This Goal Achievable: This is a critical question to ascertain whether this goal is actually achievable? You don't want to write down goals that you know you cannot achieve. Before you finalize the goal, you want to make sure you have clearly answered this question. Don't be afraid to ask yourself this question; if the question is no don't include it. It is as simple as that. So be honest with yourself and don't be afraid or feel guilty about a goal you know you can't achieve. It is best not to even set the goal, rather than to set yourself up for failure or defeat.

Steps to Overcoming Obstacles: Along the way, there will be obstacles that may cause you to fall off or be distracted. Take time to explore any obstacles that may arise. This will enable you to foresee them, as much as you can, and to include a contingency plan that will keep you on track. If something happens or you realize that the goal is no longer possible, abandon it or revise it. That is why you try to foresee as many obstacles as possible, so you can include contingencies as you move forward toward your objective.

Goal Due Date: This is the deadline date for the overall goal and not the incremental goals. Each incremental goal will have its own due date. You must identify a date when the goal, including every incremental goal, will be completed. Do your very best to adhere to this goal. Don't keep moving it. Make it a firm goal that is not easily movable and not a soft goal that can easily be changed. Remember true deadlines, don't move. Soft goals can be a major contributor to you not staying focused on the goal. Firm goals are cast in stone. Do everything possible to respect your goal's due dates by completing the incremental goals prior to or on that date.

Date Goal was Achieved: This is important because it enables you to celebrate the completion of the goal. It provides you with a sense of accomplishment. One accomplishment leads you to another and another. Yes, celebrate the completion of the goal. Celebration of your goals is an incentive for you to be even more committed to goal setting.

Did I Allot Enough Time to Achieve the Goal: This is an important question because you don't want to become discouraged if the due date comes and you have not factored in sufficient time for the goal to be achieved. Be realistic about every task that needs to be completed leading up to the completion of the ultimate goal. The incremental goals within the overall goal becomes extremely important as you allocate sufficient time for the overall goal to be achieved. Working backward from the overall goal will help you determine whether the goal is achievable within the allotted timeframe.

Comments: Include any comments that you deem to be important. This includes any motivational statements that will keep you focused. You can also include notes along the way to achieving the goal.

GOAL

DATE:

Goal Category:

Physical: To establish healthy eating habits.

Scripture reference:

1 Corinthians 6:12-13a

Steps to achieve goals:

1. Transform my thoughts about food.

2. Eat smaller portions and make better food selections—more fruit and vegetables, nuts and grains.

3. Stop feeling as though the days that I fast I am depriving myself of food, but look at it as a time of refreshing, renewal and intimacy with God. Focus on spiritual food and less on natural food.

4. Start cooking more and learning how to cook healthy and quick meals.

Is this goal achievable:

Yes, It takes a lot of self-control and discipline, especially when it comes to portion size.

Steps to overcome obstacles to achieve your goal:

Drink water before I eat. Stop feeling as though I have to eat large amounts of food at one time. Plan my meals in order that I will be able to establish and maintain a healthy lifestyle. Read books and other materials on establishing and maintaining a healthy lifestyle.

Goal due date:

Ongoing

Date goal was achieved:

Have I allotted enough time to achieve this goal:

Yes, this is a lifetime goal. For me to be healthy this has to be my lifestyle and not a diet.

Comments:

GOAL

DATE:

Goal Category:	**Professional:** Publish my book— *I DECIDED: Moving from Resolution to Execution.*
Scripture reference:	Jeremiah 30:2, Psalm 45:1
Steps to achieve goals:	1. Develop an outline that includes introductory chapters
	2. Continue researching content for introductory chapters
	3. Write the introductory chapters
	4. Finalize Goal setting section
	5. Finalize copy
	6. Give to editor
	7. Identify a printing/publishing company
Is this goal achievable:	Yes, it is achievable if I utilize my time wisely, stay focused and do something every day. Write every day.
Steps to overcome obstacles to achieve your goal:	Set a side the allotted time to complete the assignments.
Goal due date:	December 31, _____
Date goal was achieved:	December 20, _____
Have I allotted enough time to achieve this goal:	Yes, I have allotted enough time to achieve this goal.
Comments:	

GOAL

DATE:

Goal Category:

_____

Scripture reference:

_____

Steps to achieve goals:

_____

Is this goal achievable:

_____

Steps to overcome obstacles to achieve your goal:

_____

Goal due date:

_____

Date goal was achieved:

_____

Have I allotted enough time to achieve this goal:

_____

Comments:

_____

I DECIDED

GOAL

DATE:

Goal Category:

_____

Scripture reference:

_____

Steps to achieve goals:

_____

Is this goal achievable:

_____

Steps to overcome obstacles
to achieve your goal:

_____

Goal due date:

_____

Date goal was achieved:

_____

Have I allotted enough time
to achieve this goal:

_____

Comments:

_____

GOAL

DATE:

Goal Category:

_____

Scripture reference:

_____

Steps to achieve goals:

_____

_____

_____

_____

Is this goal achievable:

_____

Steps to overcome obstacles to achieve your goal:

_____

Goal due date:

_____

Date goal was achieved:

_____

Have I allotted enough time to achieve this goal:

_____

Comments:

_____

GOAL

DATE:

Goal Category:

_____

_____

Scripture reference:

_____

_____

Steps to achieve goals:

_____

Is this goal achievable:

_____

Steps to overcome obstacles to achieve your goal:

_____

Goal due date:

_____

Date goal was achieved:

_____

Have I allotted enough time to achieve this goal:

_____

Comments:

_____

GOAL

DATE:

Goal Category:

_____

Scripture reference:

_____

Steps to achieve goals:

_____

Is this goal achievable:

_____

Steps to overcome obstacles
to achieve your goal:

_____

Goal due date:

_____

Date goal was achieved:

_____

Have I allotted enough time
to achieve this goal:

_____

Comments:

_____

I DECIDED

GOAL

DATE:

Goal Category:
_____

_____

Scripture reference:
_____

_____

Steps to achieve goals:

_____

Is this goal achievable:
_____

_____

Steps to overcome obstacles to achieve your goal:
_____

Goal due date:
_____

Date goal was achieved:
_____

Have I allotted enough time to achieve this goal:
_____

Comments:
_____

_____

GOAL

DATE:

Goal Category:

_____

Scripture reference:

_____

Steps to achieve goals:

_____

Is this goal achievable:

_____

Steps to overcome obstacles
to achieve your goal:

_____

Goal due date:

_____

Date goal was achieved:

_____

Have I allotted enough time
to achieve this goal:

_____

Comments:

_____

GOAL

DATE:

Goal Category:

_____

Scripture reference:

_____

Steps to achieve goals:

_____

Is this goal achievable:

_____

Steps to overcome obstacles
to achieve your goal:

_____

Goal due date:

_____

Date goal was achieved:

_____

Have I allotted enough time
to achieve this goal:

_____

Comments:

_____

GOAL

DATE:

Goal Category:

_____

_____

Scripture reference:

_____

_____

Steps to achieve goals:

_____

Is this goal achievable:

_____

**Steps to overcome obstacles
to achieve your goal:**

_____

Goal due date:

_____

Date goal was achieved:

_____

**Have I allotted enough time
to achieve this goal:**

_____

Comments:

_____

GOAL

DATE:

Goal Category:

_____

Scripture reference:

_____

Steps to achieve goals:

_____

Is this goal achievable:

_____

Steps to overcome obstacles
to achieve your goal:

_____

Goal due date:

_____

Date goal was achieved:

_____

Have I allotted enough time
to achieve this goal:

_____

Comments:

_____

GOAL

DATE:

Goal Category:

_____

Scripture reference:

_____

Steps to achieve goals:

_____

_____

Is this goal achievable:

_____

Steps to overcome obstacles
to achieve your goal:

_____

Goal due date:

_____

Date goal was achieved:

_____

Have I allotted enough time
to achieve this goal:

_____

Comments:

_____

I DECIDED

GOAL

DATE:

Goal Category:

_____

Scripture reference:

_____

Steps to achieve goals:

_____

Is this goal achievable:

_____

Steps to overcome obstacles
to achieve your goal:

_____

Goal due date:

_____

Date goal was achieved:

_____

Have I allotted enough time
to achieve this goal:

_____

Comments:

_____

GOAL

DATE:

Goal Category:

_____

Scripture reference:

_____

Steps to achieve goals:

_____

Is this goal achievable:

_____

Steps to overcome obstacles
to achieve your goal:

_____

Goal due date:

_____

Date goal was achieved:

_____

Have I allotted enough time
to achieve this goal:

_____

Comments:

_____

Kudos! You've made it through the first week and you were successful. Now that you have a point of reference, you can use the Goal Setting Template to write down the larger goals you want to achieve. You can determine the timeframe to achieve these goals. Some of your goals will be ongoing because you will have to do them repeatedly like exercising, tithing, paying your bills, etc. Other goals will have a definitive timeline to be completed, such as writing a book, hosting an event, writing a business plan, etc.

As you continue to adopt goal setting as part of your life, remember there are goals within the goals. Make sure you include those as incremental steps to achieving your goals. These are the nuggets that encourage you to stay focused on the larger goal. Celebrate those goals within the goals, because they are critical to you staying the course. For instance, if you are looking to lose 50 pounds, include in your incremental steps milestones for every 10 pounds lost. Celebrate those milestones as though you have reached your goal. These mini-celebratory events will bolster your commitment and confidence in achieving the overall goal.

If you have a goal to write a book, you need to include every step beginning with research, organizing the information, writing, editing, identifying a publisher, sending the manuscript to the editor, sending the manuscript to the copyright office, sending it to the graphic designer, etc. Every one of these goals has a date for completion. These are the goals within the goals. Without them, you would not have a yardstick to adequately measure whether you are doing what is necessary to achieve the overall goal. After you have completed the goal, re-evaluate the goal to determine if there are subsequent goals. Almost every goal will not end when you complete the overall goal. You are forever changing and evolving as well. Keep this in mind, so you can continue in the direction of fulfillment of your goals.

Goals are dynamic! They are forever evolving because you are forever evolving. Every goal you set will more than likely have subsequent goals. For instance, you set a goal to start a business. You do everything necessary to start the business along with every incremental goal within the goal. You've finally filed all the papers, got incorporated, identified your name, and registered with the local, state and national governments. You completed the initial step to start the business, but now you must write goals for operating the business and to move the business forward.

Using the ideas shared above, take time to write down your goals and find someone whom you can trust to share them with for accountability. When you identify someone to be accountable they will help you stay on the right path. I recommend you seek someone who is unafraid to be critically honest with you. You don't need someone who is going to go along with your actions or inactions. You need someone who is going to be compassionately forceful in helping you to stay on track and prod forward.

AN EXTRA PUSH

All of us make resolutions and set goals. Sometimes we are not successful in reaching them. Having someone to help you break through barriers you may or may not be able to do on your own, can make the difference in your success. In our quest to be true to the vows we make, there are times when you need that extra push and that extra support. I know I do!

When I lived with one of my sisters in Washington D.C., my mother charged us with looking after each other. She told my sister to take care of me because I was her baby sister, and she told me to listen to and look out for my sister because she was my big sister. She essentially made us accountable to each other. Over the nine years we lived together we did just that. Howbeit, my sister would take it way too serious. Often, I had to remind her that just because she was a Captain in the Army did not mean I was under her command. Reflecting over those years I appreciate her constant urgings and support. It caused me to stretch and do things I probably never would have done. Accountability makes you do things you don't want to do, but sometimes you need someone to give you a nudge, if not a shove, to keep you moving forward.

When you identify someone to stand with you, make sure they are truly going to hold you accountable and are trustworthy, honest and can provide compassionate support. Conversely, they cannot be apprehensive about telling you when you are messing up. They must be able to speak the unadulterated truth, regardless of how painful it may be. Remember they have your best interest at heart. So, after you mull over your hurt feelings, settle down and listen. It is for your own good.

HAVE A PEP RALLY ME!

I gave myself pep talks all the time. Whenever I felt as though I was not making the mark, I would assess the situation and give myself a pep talk to do better. Now I could tell you that it always worked. In some cases it did and in others it didn't. I knew that if I continued to encourage myself, I would never give up because giving up was no longer an option.

When you give up on yourself is when all hope is lost. It doesn't matter if others give up on you, that is their prerogative. When you give up on yourself then you are headed for trouble. If you can't encourage yourself, you are destined for failure. Encouraging yourself is critical for your success. Others can provide you with words of encouragement. At some point, you must know how to encourage yourself by embracing those words as your own. If not, when you gaze in the mirror the reflection others see will in no way resemble the distorted reflection you have of yourself. Until you can view yourself as a winner, you will not see the reflection of a winner. Your image of yourself must be in alignment with what you feel about yourself. Your belief in who you are and what is inside of you will make the difference in your success. In high school, we went to pep rallies before the game to get everyone pumped up. We cheered and screamed for the intense purpose of encouraging our team to win. Our goal was to ignite school spirit by getting behind our team. In some cases, the teams weren't really winners, but we still cheered them on in hopes that this game would make the difference. Die-hard fans don't care if the team wins or not, they are still going to cheer with them in hopes that the next game will be the big win.

Who is in your cheering circle? Right now, you are probably running down a litany of people. That is the most natural thing to do. You begin to think about all the people who support you, your dreams and your goals. How many have you listed at this point? Wow! You never knew this many people believed in you. That's great!

Where on the list do you fall? If you didn't say at the top, then you need to re-evaluate your list. There comes a time when the only people at the pep rally are "me, myself and I." In essence, you are the only crowd there. No one else is around to encourage you. No one is there to cheer you on. You can't even reach the most reliable person who will tell you how great you are.

This is where the rubber meets the road. It is when you need to host a pep rally for yourself as you cheer yourself to victory. It is at this moment when you need to know that your pep rally is working. It is then that your words are the very tools used to encourage you to keep moving. Mama wasn't there, and neither was Daddy. Your sister wasn't there, and your brother was missing from action as well. You feel like the mantra my family and I teasingly said to each other as youngsters, "You ain't got no friends." Every friend you thought you had has disappeared into obscurity.

Oh, but you got yourself. Until you learn to like you, you will never be able to be your own cheering squad. You will always seek outside stimulus to speak words of life in you. In actuality, until you learn to cheer for and believe in yourself, the words of others fall on stony ground. They never go deep enough into the very essence of your being to germinate and produce a healthy attitude.

There comes a time when you must encourage yourself. No one else can do it. It may seem as though you're a little crazy, but crazy works. Stepping out and taking a risk, requires a certain amount of crazy ambition.

I often tell people I am harder on myself than anyone else. They always look at me puzzled. You see, I am only with them a little while, but I'm with me all the time. No one knows my strengths and weaknesses better than I do. No one knows how to encourage me better than I do. The same goes for you. You know you better than anyone else. You also know what will inspire you to keep moving forward and to not give up.

You can do the same for yourself. Begin by looking in the mirror and decide to see the greatness God envisioned. If you don't know the words to say initially, there is a Book chocked-full of positive Words all about you. It's the BIBLE! I've heard that it is referred to as Basic Instructions Before Leaving Earth. You have been equipped with a mighty force, the Word of God, to propel you to succeed. Incorporate it into every goal. For it to be successful, you also have to believe it.

Making the decision to fulfilling your goals is critical—becoming sick and tired of not fulfilling your goals is the incentive that will catapult you forward. Just like I was weary of writing goals down without any success until I adopted this principle to help me, you will have to come to that same place of reckoning.

I DECIDED has been instrumental for me and others. Each day I moved from a place of resolution to an empowering place of execution. I know it will do the same for you. You just must make up your mind that no longer will your goals be mere words on paper, but they will leap off the paper and take life as you operate in Diligence, Excellence, Confidence, Integrity, Enthusiasm and Dedication that propel you from resolution to execution.

EPILOGUE

B efore I adopted I DECIDED to move me from a place of just writing resolution after resolution without any evidence of them becoming a reality, I didn't experience the success I do today. These seven principles, Diligence, Excellence, Confidence, Integrity, Discipline, Enthusiasm and Dedication, have helped me to realize that every day I decide to be successful. My actions dictate my success augmented by a winning attitude.

Ultimately, resolutions are mere words until you give them permission to leap off the page by putting the corresponding actions with them. It is my hope that as you meander through these seven principles, you will experience the same transformation I did, and you will begin to not just write resolutions, but you will emerge as an executor. This emergence will cause you to never again write down empty lifeless resolutions. Every goal that you set, you will begin to achieve them.

Please take a moment to share your success with me. You can visit our website at www.jassaipublishing.org to provide your own success stories as you embrace, **I DECIDED: Proven Steps to Move from Resolution to Execution.**

ABOUT THE AUTHOR
Jacqui A. Showers

Business Encouragement Coach Jacqui Showers provides a collaborative integrated holistic approach to empower, equip and develop spirit-centered leaders and individuals to be effective change agents in an ever-evolving marketplace for purposeful spiritual, professional and personal living. Showers' bold, in-your-face style is not for the faint at heart. She encourages, equips and empowers you to become all God envisioned so you can experience what God S.A.W.W. (Spiritual, Abundance, Wholeness & Wealth).

She is the visionary and founder of JASSAI LLC, JASSAI Publishing, The ME Place Mentor Empowerment Institute, and The Showers Group Ministries. Showers hosts an annual conference, Oh Break Out Empowerment & Leadership Experience, which equips and empowers individuals to seamlessly integrate spirituality with the reality of the marketplace. Showers shares practical empowering, life-transforming principles during her weekly empowerment hour, *11:59 A Minute 'til Midnight Marketplace* Prayer Boot Camp. She also distributes a daily Prayer for Success to an extensive email subscriber list and on her social media platforms. Through her writings, Showers has the unique ability to transform basic life experiences into powerful lessons for illimitable success.

A sought-after speaker, Showers provides unboxed coaching for unboxed success through individual consultations, workshops, seminars, webinars, conferences, books, blogs, and e-blasts for personal, spiritual, professional, business, and leadership development. As a Kingdom solutionist and a marketplace leader with substantial experience in management, business development and marketing communications, Showers has provided consultation, strategic oversight, management and leadership to non-profits, government, corporations and small businesses.

Showers is an ordained Elder serving at House of Prayer & Praise Ministries and provides leadership for the Intercessory Prayer Ministry and serves on the Ministerial Alliance. She is a graduate of Wayne State University and resides in Detroit, Michigan.

Showers holds dear the love affair she and God share that's totally beyond compare and her commitment to a consecrated life rooted in prayer, fasting and the Word of God.

Connect with her on Twitter @ShowersBlessing, Facebook, LinkedIn, Instagram, Periscope and Pinterest. Visit www.theshowersgroupministries.org and www.jassaipublishing.com to become a subscriber with her.

OTHER WORKS FROM THE AUTHOR

Prayers for Success: Igniting the World to Achieve Success

Prayers for Success: Igniting the World to Achieve Success has been created to reach beyond the four walls of church into the wall-less-ness of the marketplace. These bold succinct prayers can be prayed in 60 seconds or less. They are prayers for the information age. Each prayer is virtually 500 characters or less addressing every area of life—spiritually, professionally, financially, personally, physically, relationally, environmentally and socially. From encouragement to live out your passion, to increasing your relationship with God, to strengthening your relationships with others, to managing your business, to establishing a healthy lifestyle, to managing money, to overcoming the loss of a loved one and more, *Prayers for Success: Igniting the World to Achieve Success* is written to empower and encourage the total individual to embrace the prosperous life God envisioned.

Affirmations for Success: Daily Affirmations for Marketplace Influencers

Words frame our world. Words transform our mindsets. Words are filtered through our eye-gates and ear-gates into our brains and move down to the heart. We are the gatekeepers of our words and our hearts. Out of the heart, the mouth speaks. *Affirmations for Success: Daily Affirmations for Marketplace Influencers* provides you daily affirming words igniting you to achieve illimitable success. Each affirmation propels you to experience massive transformation. *Affirmations for Success'* self-affirming words are touch stones, when applied every day will transform your mind, environment and relationships to experience the abundant life God envisioned.

BIBLIOGRAPHY

Batterson, Mark. 2011. The Circle Maker: Praying Circles Around Your Biggest Dreams and Greatest Fears. Grand Rapids, MI: Zondervan. n.d. Famous Quotes at BrainyQuote. Accessed October 4, 2018. https://www.brainyquote.com/.n. d.

Inside The Huddle. Accessed October 4, 2018. http://www.insidethehuddle.tv/articles/top-10-most-memorable-quotes-vince-lombardi. n. d. Famous Quotes at BrainyQuote. Accessed October 4, 2018. https://www.brainyquote.com/.

"Nathaniel Bronner Jr. Quotes." n.d. ThinkExist.com. ThinkExist. Accessed October 4, 2018. http://thinkexist.com/quotation/no-one-will-question-your-integrity-if-your/1133169.html.

New Century Version. Nashville: Thomas Nelson Publishers, 1987. Peterson, Eugene H. The Message. NavPress, 2002.

The Holy Bible, King James Version. Philadelphia: National Publishing Company, 1987.

The Holy Bible, New King James Version. Nashville: Thomas Nelson Publishers, 1982.

The Living Bible. Wheaton: Tyndale Publishers, 1971.

The New American Standard Bible, La Habra: Lockman Foundation, 1995.

The New International Version. Grand Rapids: Zondervan, 2011. Thoreau, Henry David. Walden. New York: Thomas Y. Crowell & Co, 1854.

CPSIA information can be obtained
at www.ICGtesting.com
Printed in the USA
FFHW021920241119
56124363-62235FF